Silent Kingdom

By E.B. Allen

Dedication

To my darling daughter, Claire. Thank you for pushing me, always, to put myself out there. You are braver than you think, and stronger than you can ever imagine. You will conquer this world and do amazing things! Never fear the unknown, for in the unknown we often find our true self.

CONTENTS

In a world full of so many opinions and voices trying to tell me which way to go... I often find my true voice in the silence. Yet, it is far too often in the silence brought about by others that we learn to endure pain and heartache. Not all silences can be felt, but the ones we feel deep down to our core... those are the ones that turn our stomachs upside-down. Those are the ones that keep us up at night. Those are the ones worth writing about.

ACKNOWLEDGMENTS

Thank you to Jesse Murawski (Instagram: jessie.m.art) for the beautiful cover art. You are like a second daughter to me and I can never thank you enough for being such an amazing light in both of our lives.

I'm not looking for a quick fuck, nor an easy fuck. Conversate me. Look me in the eyes and follow through. Learn about me, not ignore me. You wanna fuck? Then dive into the forest of my mind and grab ahold. Go for a ride that will mean something in the morning and not be simply something you regret. Don't fuck me because I am there. Anyone can be there. Want me because I am different, and you want it all. I'm not an easy fuck. I don't wanna be anyone's quick anything. You wanna see a forest shine? Let's talk.

I still feel like nothing. Despite your making me actually feel something today. Yet, that something is actually nothing. Will never be anything. I feel stupid for even a nanosecond of thinking of something more than what is there. Where there actually isn't even a *there* – there. At least not for you. I'm not even sure if I can feel anything again. Even if there was a there, the darkness broke me long ago. Still… the brief thought of it with you was pleasant. The moment passed. Won't return. Alone I lay here in bed just glad to have even met you. I need nothing more than that. Because I, myself, am nothing.

In all of the darkness that surrounds me, I cannot help but feel you. Feel your goodness. Something about the way you speak, reminds me of who I used to be. Before I knew how dark the world really was. Before all the pain and sadness. I want to grab ahold of you before you understand why you shouldn't be here. I want something I cannot have, and that alone is enough to drive anyone a little mad at first. Yet, I've grown so accustomed to being alone that I am numb to the pain of any thoughts of losing you. You aren't even here. A perpetual figment of my imagination is where my feelings for you live. Never to be real – like grasping for a dream when waking in the middle of the night. You can feel it so strongly, but it isn't real. That is where I will have to hold you... deep inside my mind.

I often imagine the pain of kissing you. That you probably taste like fear. Your past haunting every moment of my tongue pressed against yours. Hands pressed against unfamiliar flesh. Leading you to pull away. Pause and rethink. Killing the moment. Killing your desires. Destroying any future moments. Walking away unsatisfied. Leaving a lasting taste of your fear in my mouth.

Don't take this away from me. The pain that comes with the bitter taste of my reality. The lies that you tell are so convincing. Hitting me softly like a sweet kiss on the lips. When you really are stabbing me in the heart. Hiding who you really are and what you are really about. Stealing moments of my time just to feed your ego and misogynistic ways. I felt every word. Hung onto everything you said as if it should matter to me. Oblivion is your entire being. That is my parting gift to you.

I'm stuck. Not the kind of stuck you struggle to escape from out of fear or pain. This is the kind that eats away at your insides because you know you can never have what is right in front of you. When you can only look from a distance. The kind that creates a desire to totally fuck your mind over. Because there is no way to change where you are at. You can never move forward or backwards even. There is nothing you can do but watch as the world ticks around you. Watch as nothing happens in your life, but everything happens to others. Stuck. I am completely and totally stuck.

The darkness of my mind never lets me crave you for too long. Always beckoning me back to the shadows, where I feel safe. I try to crawl out for longer each time. Wanting you to become a part of me, yet unable to obtain even a piece of your love. The darkness will never allow me to feel your heart beating next to mine. It would never let me get too close to you. I can never leave. There is no escape.

Your words spoke to a part of me that had been lost.
Now that I've found it, I need more than words.

Many have tried to see that side of me, but you are the only one I felt safe enough to show it to. Shame it was wasted on something so fleeting.

I wake up missing you
Dreams so deeply felt
Your hands on my skin
Your kiss so passionate
Words gently whispered
Dreams so deeply felt
I miss what isn't real

It is infinitely possible
You take me away
To places undiscovered
Deep in the darkness
A single spark of light
Your words penetrate
Resonating within me
Stirring up trouble
For something
So well hidden

There is a path to my world
You must take each step with care
And without expectation of arriving anywhere soon
If you stumble I will catch you
If you skip a step
You will fail to reach your destination
The journey is not for those seeking anything
Other than truth and honest love

My darkest thoughts never imagine your face
Not perfectly
Shadows will dance around and laugh and say
Not today
Behind your mask I dare to peek
Fear will not allow
You are lost inside my head
Trapped in the void just beyond the darkness
You are beyond reach; yet my mind knows you
Wants you
Your face haunts me every night
Despite not having met you yet

There is a sweet symphony inside my head as I lay awake wondering wildly about you. Never met, never known. Still I dream. Too much darkness surrounds this fog. Breaking free, running wild among the trees. Kiss me softly as I slumber deeply. For when I wake, you will be gone once again.

Hovering over the words I wish to speak
Erasing slowly the bitter taste of fear
Licking chops like lollipops
Struggling to jump outside of this world
City lights so far from reality
I lean, I push, I leap
Floating weightlessly outside my mind
Phrases I dare not speak

Falling
Is that good or bad?
I do not want to fall alone
Do you understand?
Or am I alone in that too?

Even if I never say a word
You notice what I am saying
The darkness that keeps us both alive at night
Is the same one that makes us understand the
silence
It seeps into our minds
Madness some might call it
We cannot escape it
Yet we fight these demons as If we can

Your words sink inside me
I crave more
I desire your touch
A longing to feel you
To have you next to me
To feel your words
Slowly drifting inside my ear
As your hands softly touch me

The worst part about this feeling
I cannot stop it
It will run straight through me
Like an unstoppable train
I will lose my breath
Feel torn into pieces
And you...
You will walk away unscathed

There aren't enough goodbyes
To express how I will miss you
Instead, I will simply slip away
From your thoughts
From your mind
From your life
I will cherish every bit of you
Until I forget how it feels to long for you
Until the scars on my heart heal
Until my very last breath

Words feed me
You find a way
To starve me
Keeping me wanting
Longing for more
A hunger like no other
Feed me your words
Satisfy me

I am not sure if I am running away
Or towards you
Longing for something
My thoughts return to you
Again, and again
Waking in the night
I lay there
Mind wandering
Wanting
Desiring
Dreams that keep me awake

Do not tempt me with a belief that your illusions of being something that you are not are real. If I can smudge your edges, they are not solid. If I can erase all that you pretend to be, it is not valid. If a breeze can change your course so quickly, you are not worthy. If my grasp upon your hand cannot be felt within every fiber of our bodies, then it should not happen. Not like this, not now, not ever. I am not the girl you see on paper. I am flesh and blood with a desire which can only be satisfied by someone brave enough to be real.

Go silently.
Sneak away and let your absence in the night
Be your greatest love story
Do not let the darkness frighten you away
Dreams live in the shadows
Where your demons once played
Take hold of that feeling
Let it feed you
Stop sinking
Swim to the surface
Take a breath and live
Live!

They are only words
How can I feel them?
Want them?
Crave them?
Understanding you
Is the hardest lesson
Learning more
Is the only thing
That I want
Which is why
I cannot have it

You are my favorite thought
And the reason for
Chills that run down my spine
When my mind wonders
To places it should not go

I don't want to be alone
With my thoughts
Not anymore
I crave sharing them
With someone else
Someone wanting
To hear my thoughts
To feel me lying next to them
As I speak from the heart
Telling stories of you and me
And love created from past hurt
But found amongst the rubble
Was something worth keeping
Can I tell you a story?

You were the one to ignite
A spark inside the darkness
The flame burnt fiercely
Quickly
You were the one to flicker
Extinguishing the fire within
Darkness

Truth is so simple
Do not feed me lies
Just to satisfy my hunger
You already had my attention
Now clouded in darkness
Never to find the light again
Once tainted, always lost

I have been lost inside a reflection
Trying to become someone else
For someone else
The person looking back at me
Isn't me
I'm tired of carnival reflections
Distorting my image
Contorting my view
For someone like you
Someone who wouldn't know true beauty
Could never hold
The depths of a person's mind
So deep and unattainable
By hands that let go so easily

You felt like tomorrow
Something unattainable
Like a dream you cannot hold onto
Crazy notions of futures to be had
Instead...
It was history repeating
Not new
Not better
Not real
Nothing prepared my heart
For you
Sliced open before I had a chance
To breathe you in
To sink my teeth into your flesh
Feel your heart beating
Now you feel like sorrow
Someone to run from
Learn from
Grow from

Stop me before I fall
I whisper under breath
Knowing fully
I cannot stop
I am already gone
Lost in thoughts
Of love
Of touching
Of experiencing
Everything about you

I do not want to know
How to lose you
I am not looking
For pain
I will never understand anyone
Who can walk away
After one night
After one moment
After one connection
Loving is too deep
To just vanish
Forever into the night

My heart is melting for a person I hardly know. The strangest sensation is knowing that they have no idea how amazing they are in my opinion. Even weirder is that they will probably never understand what I see in them.

The harder I love your mind
The more I want your body
Feed me your knowledge
Allow me to feast
And never go hungry again

A beautiful mind is very attractive to me. Share all your thoughts with me and I will love you even more.

Never mistake my kindness
For something greater
I am kind to everyone
Never mistake my words
For something deeper
I speak volumes to everyone
If I show you a side
Meant for someone special
Then I am speaking only
To you
If you mistake that for less
Then you will lose
Something even greater

Always diving in
Head first
To life
To love
Quick to feel
The broken path
To life
To love
She will never
Give up
On life
On love

Take me away
Somewhere far
Unrecognizable
Just us
No static
Nothing
Enjoy me
As I enjoy
You
Take me away
To love you more
Than ever before
Just us
Nothing
Taste me
As I taste
You
Take me away

When you try to put something or someone out of your mind, but you constantly see reminders of them in everything you do... it makes it harder to leave thoughts of them behind. Maybe life wants you to keep them there, or perhaps you do.

The deeper my thoughts go towards losing you, the more my heart aches. You weren't meant to last long, but here I am wondering why you left so soon.

I knew that opening up my heart again was a risk. I'm glad it was with you, and I'm glad to have felt something for someone so wonderful.

The empty nights make missing you that much harder. Your love filled the darkness making it almost feel like a place I could understand. This quiet only gives my mind room to think... and all I seem to think about is you.

Fighting off the power that addictions have over me tonight. Even love is addicting. I know this because my love for you is the strongest addiction I have felt yet.

If giving away a piece of my heart to another person means it might break and burn into a pile of ash and ruin... I will take that chance every damn time. Always choose to give love to someone... even strangers you may never see again.

My timing is always wrong, or perhaps it is because I am impossible to love?

My heart spoke in a rhythm that I thought you understood. Each time we spoke you hit all the right notes. Now I just feel played. Used for my song so that your soul felt soothed for a bit. Without you around, my rhythm feels off, I feel like I am out of tune.

There were so many things I wanted you to know. You left my life as swiftly as you came. Quiet like a ninja. Only it is I who is left to fight off the demons alone. The haunting memories of what we could have been... if only you stayed.

A frequency of static
No more turns on the dial
The volume has all but gone
Fading away slowly
I reach for you
Nothing but dead air
Where once played
A beautiful melody
Of our love

If my words cannot change your mind to stay in my life, just a little longer, then I am lost. For words are the only thing I have to get me through this world. If you do not want them, I will let them float into the world and drift into oblivion, until there is silence.

I would rather be poor and in love than wealthy and alone.

The memory of your voice echoes inside my head as the night grows quiet.

Haunting my darkest nights with your silence.

I fell on your every word like a dagger through the heart. Splitting me open with each new line. Catching a glimpse of your ego. Your words quickly soured. Never to be felt the same way again.

I imagine slaying a dragon would be easier than loving me. This must be why no one has even tried in so long. Are there no valiant men?

I would rather be marked as crazy for loving too deeply then sane for being unable to truly love.

My days are filled with noise, my nights with silence. Burden me with your noise so that I may feel something warm in the cold dark night.

You existed before I knew you and you will exist long after we part, but when we are together... that is something not to exist again.

There have been too many moments stolen by darkness, by pain, and by misery. Your moments were lovely. I did not understand this until they were gone.

Are there words to save a wounded soul?

There was this pause in our chatter
And in that simple moment
My heart skipped a beat
Because I knew what that meant
You would not be around much longer

Thoughts of feeling your body close to mine are only enough if the thoughts eventually turn into actions.

You cannot place a value on a loving heart. Some toss it away like garbage. Others pretend it does not exist. A great many live in fear of the notion. If you are lucky enough to have another love you... a great many envy that. Do not dismiss it so easily.

I am not sure which feeling is worse... knowing you are gone... or realizing that it was not at all what it seemed?

Impale me with your words so that I may forget about everything else in this world.

She hid behind her fears, wanting to feel something greater than the walls surrounding her world. So, she went out searching...

I had two dreams last night, and for the first time in a long while… you were not in them. I'm not sure if I'm grateful or sad? I'm still miss you either way.

Sleep comes at a price. How am I to get over you... if your love still haunts my dreams?

I heard you screaming in the silence. Louder than anything you ever spoke before. I learned from silence.

How savage of this world to allow us to believe in love so quickly. A pill, a potion, or even a notion of something to stop us from falling before we should.

What pain is this that feels like a dagger? No wound upon my flesh. No poison have I sipped. You leave, and I am to die inside? Your lips that I used to dream of kissing. Your eyes that longingly looked upon me now look elsewhere. Silence now feels so deadly.

My words flow freely from my heart, but never reach their intended destination. Forever to float about this earth; unfelt, unknown, unwanted... by you.

What if I let go? Drift away slowly into the void between the realities of love and hate, be numb to it all, would I be happy?

Your words touched me in places my mind had not seen before. I miss those places the most.

Words can still be felt, long after they have gone.
Choose your words carefully.

If I told you I was starving for the taste of your lips...
and this confuses you... there is not a lot I will say
that you will understand.

I was afraid you would become a yes, so I said no first to save myself that pain. Every yes turns into a no eventually... so why dive deeper into the abyss?

I used to wear the biggest smile when you spoke. You could have read me the label on a box. I was yours for the taking... I no longer smile when you speak.

You were a distraction from my life. A beautiful, yet simple distraction. I miss being distracted, but I am not sure I miss you.

She wanted to be found by someone worthy of knowing her deepest thoughts. He spoke to a part of her that she had almost forgotten about. She let him in... one breath at a time. It was not easy for her, but she was up for the challenge.

All of a sudden... you meant nothing more to me than words on a screen. Ones and zeros transmitting at high speed used to bring so much joy. Lost in the code somewhere along the way... were my feelings for you.

I turned the page and realized half-way down... you are no longer part of my story.

I thought fate had whispered your name
A temptation dangled in front of me
Vanishing quickly into oblivion
Never to be heard from again
Fate laughed and replied
No, not him

Words that spoke lies and silences that spoke truths.

I loved feeling like I meant something to someone. You are gone now, and you took that feeling with you.

I was once happy inside the haze of your words.

Lay here with me in silence. Let the soft sounds of our breath feed the night.

You flung your words at me. Aiming straight for my heart. I was onto you. Still, I let you take your aim, each and every time. Never missing. Until one day you put down your bow and walked away. I still have arrows in me. Some broken. Some burnt.

I have spent many nights dreaming of you. Your voice, your hands, and your love. Until I woke up and realized that you were just a dream. Never to be real.

When this drug called love wears off... I will be myself again, only a little torn.

You were a mistake, but I enjoyed every fucking second of it.

Repeating history. Lessons never learned. Twisted up.
Wanting an escape from this, what will end in misery.
Always ending. Not enough beginning. But damn I
love the middle. Never enough of that to go around.
Soft and beautiful messes. I'd kill for that.

My mistakes do not make me any less. I feed on every bit of noise you toss at me. Static that fills my mind with words. I beg for silence to bring out every word you shouted. To echo for hours after. Driving my pen to write even faster; deeper.

The darkness is heavy today.

I let myself become a part of you. Your words let me believe in something, believe in you. Now a hollowed-out vessel, searching for words to fill what you emptied out. Every word, every sound, every note of music feels like drops in the ocean without your presence.

You watch me, as if you know me
Speak, as if you care
...
...
...
...
...
You will never know me
I'm not a book for you to read
You can keep your fake words
I will make my own words flow together
To sooth my tired soul

The lies you spin are a beautiful web of disaster that trap me every time. You drain me almost dry and set me free just to trap me again later to feed upon once again. Isn't your ego full yet?

My love for you was once shiny and new. You ignored me and left me outside too long. Despite your wanting me to move for you now, I cannot. My gears have rusted from exposure to the elements. My color has all but faded away. I can no longer be used by you.

Desires you will never satisfy
Lay deep within me
Where the air is thin
And hard to breathe
Suffocating my mind
With your poisonous words
Black tears fall
All around my feet
Swallowing me up
Inside my own darkness

The weight of your words
Too heavy for me
Pulling me down
Under a darkened sky
Reaching for the light
Of a million stars
Shining so far away
Unreachable
As you are now
A distance unattainable
By mere steps forward
Stumbling in the darkness
Pulled down by your words

How foolish of me to have begun again. This crazy notion of love being right for me. Maybe it is all of the "you's" in this world, or perhaps it is actually me who cannot become what is needed to be loved by a single soul on this planet.

There is a deep void inside me. It is impossible to fill. Every time you leave, I try. You come back, and it feels less like a cure and more like a patch. Stitched on by lies. You always leave and manage to take more of me with you. The void is growing deeper.

A frequency of static
No more turns on the dial
The volume has all but gone
Fading away slowly
I reach for you
Nothing but dead air
Where once played
A beautiful melody
Of our love

I keep falling in love with people who turn out not to exist. Falling for the mask you wear instead of the true you.

The voice inside my head keeps holding me back. So many words left unspoken.

How long to wait for the end of time? Why am I still waiting? You are full of flaws, but only wanting perfection from others. A darkness needing quenched by a lighter soul. You intend to drag down your next victim, then leave. A dark wake behind you.

Trying not to let the darkness fall too heavily on my mind. These bitter days of loneliness, still spinning from a past I long to escape. Craving you, craving me. All too heavy. A numbness creeps inside, stays for a while. Losing touch with who I want to be.

To the weak minded, I am too much. To the strong minded, I am perfect. To you, I am nothing.

There is no distance greater than that of loss and love. The euphoria of love, and the deep darkness of losing love. Somewhere in the middle, I have been lost to the numbness of feeling nothing.

To you I am a pawn. A piece to move around the board until you are ready to make your move. Fooled by your game no longer. I have taken my leave. No longer will I be moved by your words.

I crave a poison to take away the edge beneath me. Let me float and drift above the surface for a while. A tiny taste on the tip of your lips, perhaps would be enough. Allow me to escape the darkness just this once.

I speak only from the heart. My words may have roots, thorns, or wings. Those who fear reality and extreme honesty will run away from words such as these. I'm looking for someone who isn't afraid.

I fear that if I stop thinking about you, then you will go away forever. I'm not sure I could take not knowing you. I have no idea how to make the pain stop, other than by just knowing that you exist in my world. Knowing that you are still in mine. Our little secret world.

A conversation worth remembering is a conversation I want to have. All others are pointless noise to drown out my missing your words.

I stepped on the gas, and you put on the brakes. This was the end of anything that could have been between us.

You see me as frail. I dare you to test my strength. I have endured more than you can ever imagine in your simple ego filled mind.

I have come to seek out the silence. The dark moody colors of the night. This room has nothing to offer me other than solitude. Thoughts free to flow without fear of interruptions. A darkness like no other, here alone in a bed of stillness. Silence calls my name.

I cannot haunt you anymore
You no longer need my presence
I have found another to occupy
This flesh upon my bones
Your silence gave me reasons
To listen to the space between us
Your words no longer please me
This is our goodnight, and goodbye

I allow you to play with my emotions. Do not confuse that with love. Love is not a game. I would never allow myself to fall in love with a player such as yourself. For now, I enjoy your game. Never for a moment believe you will ever win anything real from me.

You used my kindness against me
Left me hanging on a thread
Dangling high above the city
Always there for you
To play with my emotions
To feed your ego
Learning to dance on rooftops
I escaped by swinging
Fraying the thread
Until the day it broke
Setting me free

He set the stage
Acted the part
I fell in love
With the boy
With the moment
Removed the mask
Revealed the players
Lost all faith
In love
In people
Nothing is real
It's all a big scene
Dramatically painful
The curtain is falling
On another lover

I am unsure of who you see
Do you see the darkness I write
Or the light in my soul
Do you see right through me
Straight onto the next girl
Am I even seen by you
Or seen by anyone at all

Every sound reminds me of you. Drowning it all out with any noise louder than my mind. I'm not sure I have it in me. The darkness pulls too swiftly. Taking over the moments. Leaving a mark. A gentle reminder of who is winning your game.

There is no coming home from the darkness. It never let's go. Feeds on every bit of your flesh. Until your bones ache and you are crawling towards the light. Begging for a drop of love to taste... just once more before you close your eyes on this world.

Sinking deeper into a void beyond the edge of all my fears. A place once buried in the past; long forgotten. Now alive and pulling me under. Struggling to breathe. Grabbing ahold of anything solid. Trying to survive.

Walking away becomes easier with every breaking heart. A battle drum beat that begins when the last tear has fallen.

I used to escape into the thought of you. Now I barely remember what that felt like. A dream no longer desired. Your words a distant memory to an ever-fading feeling of having wanted you. Tainted by a darkness of growing silence. You are all but gone to me.

I tried to save you from destroying us. In the end, all I could do was sit back and watch you burn everything to the ground.

Her mind is deeper than the hole you dug to bury her in. Your hate and vile nature will not destroy her. Growing talons to claw through the darkness; she escaped. Head held high she kissed you farewell. Watched as you fell backwards into your own misery.

Her favorite color, black
Darkness flowed in her veins
Swallowed by the night
With stardust dancing in her eyes
She remained balanced
Never taking for granted
The hope hiding in her soul
Shining like beacons
Seeking someone to love
And to be loved in return

I escape through hidden doors and secret passages. Hidden in plain sight. Ignored by all who cannot understand the darkness. Those who fear the demons cry and scratching of the woods will never find their way. Dare to follow along. Escape with me.

Ghosts have consumed parts of me that used to be my entire world. Now just a fading shadow dancing in the back of my mind.

Suffering from the pain of this silence. The worst washed away with this spring rain. Loving you, a mistake of the winter blues. Forsaken by thoughts of finding happiness in an ego such as yours. Drowning out the world with noise and chaos.

There is a darkness to your soul that I feed upon.
Your words haunt me even as I sleep. Feeling the soft
touch of a shadow lay next to me. I awake, and you
are gone. Feelings still linger throughout the day.
Dragging me back into the night.

I will never rise up against you. Fighting battles within my own mind. Harming you will only harm me. You are not worth the pain.

She, with low cut tops and no bra on. She, with low self-esteem and nowhere else to go. She, with a look in her sexy eyes and no morals in her soul. Was it she, or your lack of self-control that tore us apart?

Suddenly you were no longer there. The hot summer heat blew through my hair as the storm kicked up. Taillights heading west. Tears heading south. No long goodbye to hold onto. Just another missing moment to exist without you.

You were important. Something I needed to get me past the darkness. A little voice telling me to fight on. I've grown into my own voice now. You are now a distraction pulling me backwards. I no longer want to go back to where you are at.

The darkness of sorrow spends its days frolicking with the shadows on the wall. Gloomy dreams that wake me in the night while you sleep deep in my heart. A thousand whispers haunting my mind. Telling me that you are not to be trusted.

Words that took my breath away
Are now gone, weren't meant to stay
Causing feelings to stir deep inside
Lies; you were cute, so I let that slide
I believed that you were different
You didn't feel the same, I can take a hint

I breathed you in, expecting you to stay... only to exhale and you were gone.

You lost a part of your existence that I fell for. I no longer recognize the person I wanted to know.

I sink the fuck into the dark void and scream out your name. No longer in excitement or a desire being satisfied, but in pain and anguish. A name that used to echo back bringing me more pleasure now comes back like a knife. Killing me again and again.

I believed in more than you. I believed in an us that could take on the world and be something never seen before. Something pure and real in a plastic filled world. Turns out I was alone in believing in both us and in you.

I did not mean to fall for you
Your precision to words
Kept my heart racing
It was my fault
I shouldn't have trusted
My own heart
Shouldn't have given it away
To someone so careless
Someone not even wanting it
Should have known better
Than wanting to feel love

This pain is determined to become the darkness that surrounds my existence. I may just let it.

An expectation
Left behind
With a realization of
Not today
Nor any other day
This Love is a
Crazy fucked up
Lessons learned
You will never be
Nor ever was
Someone meant
For me
Not to love
Nor be with
No fucking
Nor kiss goodnight
Just silence
And goodbye

I howled at you for months, but soon realize that you are not the moon. You are the darkness that surrounds it.

I traced your words like constellations in the sky.
Only to find that you were a black hole. Sucking the
life out of me.

Sometimes a small thought enters the mind and it feels like a punch in the stomach. There is no reason for this thought to have crossed your mind, yet there it is. You overthink its being there. You suffer until it's gone again.

I thought you were the cure. I swallowed down every bit of the words you spilled out. Turns out you were a poison. Slowly killing my desire to become more than this.

A burnt down memory
Etched my glass heart
Flames flicker out
Turning this, turning you
Into nothing but darkness
No more burning desires
You solidified my heart
To a stone of jade
Envious of something
I never even had

We carry on as if the end never came
As if the pain never got to us
As if we were strangers all along
No more goodnight
Never again will I feel your words
Two boats adrift at sea
You're heading east while I head west
Crashing on distant shores
Starting over, again

You were never real
I breathed you into existence
Because I needed someone
To be there for me
You slowly became a ghost
Of all my past thoughts
I filled you full
Of regrets
Of fears
Of pain
And most of all
My broken heart
...
It's hard to say goodbye
You saved me from myself
But I think it's time to let you go
To bury you with my past
There is a place in my heart and mind
Where you will always be remembered
Thank you for your love

There is action in your stillness and novels in your silence.

There are too many ghosts haunting my dreams to ever sleep through the night alone.

If I caught myself looking for something when there was nothing... perhaps there would not be all of this darkness surrounding my thoughts.

You will never feel this flesh, these bones, these eyes
gazing into yours proving how much you are worth it.

I would say that I lost something great, but I never actually had anything at all. Yet, I still feel the loss of your nothing... because you were something to me.

These conversations that used to turn me on. Now make my stomach turn. And my skin feels like ashes. Flaking off with even the slightest touch by another. You were the lava bringing heat to mold me into whatever you wanted. Without that warmth, I am not the same.

The darkness is my home. I forgot how lovely the night can be. How lovely it is to frolic with my demons and let loose all my ghosts. To once again be reminded of all the places I've been. To forget about you, I must return to a place where no one else can go.

I feel hollow
Except for the burning in my chest
That never stops
Keeps me awake
Prevents me from eating
And leaves me feeling
Numb

You left me starving
For your flesh
Creating a stir within
A void sinking deeper
Burrowing a hole
Inside my mind
You had no intention
Of fulfilling this need
Or giving me what I wanted
A game to be played
And you played it so well
With only one loser
Me

I may not have been real for you
But you were very real for me
I am allowed to feel the loss
Feel the pain
Cry the tears
Write the words
All endings are felt
I plan to feel everything
In this life
Including the loss for you

It is humbling to realize
All these thoughts
And all this time
I invested in you
Into hoping for more
Turned out to be for nothing
All your thoughts were
For her, not for me
All your time was on her
There is nothing more hurtful
Than knowing you are second
Because you were never thinking of me
Even when you were alone with me
There were thoughts of her floating by

The worst part is that I wanted every single part of you... while you wanted only one part of me.

The silence of where you used to be so loud is enough to tear me apart at times.

She was the girl who everyone cheated on. She saw in you a person who could understand what that felt like. You were the last person she thought would end up being a player. She now has stronger armor to protect herself from people like you.

I put myself out there
Gave you parts of me
That no one else would ever see
You took advantage of my weakness
Used me for what you needed
Had no intention of being more
Gave me hope where there was none
You reminded me of why I struggle
To trust anyone with any part of me
You can keep all of me that I gave you
Because I never want it back
I do not want to be reminded
Of how I will never be
Good enough for you

Moving on
Away from knowing you
From the place I wanted to be
Mostly for the sake of my own heart
Not because I no longer care
But because I still care too much
You will destroy me if I stay
And I cannot let that happen

I took you seriously
But I shouldn't have
I believed in you
But I shouldn't have
I felt something for you
But I shouldn't have
I cried for you
But I fucking shouldn't have

Ask me how I feel
The answer is simple
Numb
You took what was left
Of a broken heart
And created something new
Something different than before
I made myself believe I could be
Be a person that I hadn't been before
You took advantage of my newness
Used it for your own twisted means
Then you took it away
What you built; destroyed
I feel nothing for you now
Yet somehow everything all at once

I do not want to go back
Because back means you
Feeling something for you
All over again
I need to move forward
Without you
Because that's the only way
I can see myself healing
And being able to just carry on
You were never going to be
Anything more than this
What you are right now
You never planned to be
And I think that
That hurts most of all

I'm going to make the most
Of these horrible feelings
Turn it into beautiful words
Written to heal my heart
And perhaps maybe
Just maybe
They will heal someone else too

The cold is the only thing
Making me feel alive
The summer heat will be here soon
And it will remind me that you are gone
Your words that spoke to me deeply
In the many cold winter months
They kept me warm at night
They went away so quickly
Like the air being let out of a balloon
You left me feeling deflated
I just wanted you to breathe into me
To give me a sense of life

The sun didn't rise above the mountains today
It stayed quietly hidden behind the clouds
The darkness loomed across the entire valley
Making it even that much harder to forget about you
Maybe tomorrow the sun can cleanse my weary soul

I fought so hard inside my own head for something I thought I wanted. That something was you. Maybe I really did want you or maybe I just wanted the idea of what you represented for me. Something new. Something different and not just me being alone forever.

I thought you would make me whole
Instead you left me with a hole
Bigger than the one before
Harder to handle
More than I wanted
Leaving me questioning everything
All that I am
And all that I had become
Still not worthy
Of you
Of love

I thought I was done
Feeling
Wanting
You
The pain still lingers
Like a tiny ember
Ready to ignite
My entire world

With just the sight of you
Just a flash of a memory
And I am burning up
With sadness
With anger
With loneliness

A simple sound that still makes me look. Still makes me miss the things that you'd say. Miss the way that I felt when I saw your name. The smile that fell upon my lips. Lips I hoped one day you'd kiss. Desires that I felt for you. The things I wanted to do.

Being broken is not a valid excuse to hurt someone who cares about you.

You let me chase after you
Like a ghost
You were never really there
Like a melody
You stayed on my mind
Like a demon
You ate away at me
Until nothing was left

All that has been forgotten
Of you
And of me
Will be lost on some
But remembered by one
Etched in my mind
All the little things
About who you are
To me
You will never leave
And always have a home
Inside this beating heart

The memories of that last battle
Will forever haunt me
The screams
The pain
The loss
Changed forever
Everything about me

I thought I needed you forever
Need and want
They get confused
The heart and mind forget
Which is real and honest
Turns out I only wanted you
I do not need anyone

Darkness festering behind my step
Creeping ever closer
To my flesh
To my mind
Never letting me rest
Nor take a breath
Slowly grabbing hold
Of my body
Of my soul
Taking me places
I never wanted to go
Dragging me along
For its pleasure
For its gain
Leaving me hollow inside

You think yourself cleaver
These words that you spill
Filling up my soul
A time waster for you
A little bit more for me
You think I cannot see
These things you are doing
Filling up my mind
With images of you
With thoughts of desires
You think yourself cleaver
These emotions you twist
Filling up my dark heart

I am the person you think you want
But the one you'll never take a chance on

I could have sworn I was bulletproof
Then I met you
Now I'm riddled with holes
And dripping blood
Pouring myself out
Onto pages and film
Trying to fill in the empty spaces
With things that distract me
From the obvious pain
That is this horrifying image
Of what glances back at me
When I look into the mirror
And see what used to be me
But instead is a destroyed
Useless persona of... you

I thought perhaps it was unkind of you to turn away from someone wanting to love you... not understanding that you were incapable of being loved by someone so willing to love you.

There is a space between us that keeps filling with an empty void of silence. Who knew that silence could push so ferociously? Making it almost impossible to ever return to a place that once felt so familiar & wonderful. This silence has all but ended... us.

I snatched a moment of time with you. I felt like a badass thief each time we spoke. Knowing that our days were numbered, and I would soon have to give you back to the world. You were never meant for me to love.

It does not matter how deep my words are... you will never feel them. It does not matter how real my dreams are... you will never understand them. It does not matter how much I care for you... you will never return.

You fed my insecurities and left me wondering what was wrong with me.

I'm thrown by your definition
Of maybe
And someday
Someday was a while ago
And you still say maybe
Well, maybe isn't anywhere
No space in time I can hold
No arms to grab me
No lips to kiss me
No flesh to wrap myself around
Just empty words
And promises of nothing

I let you write yourself onto my pages
Tiny scribbles of dark ink
Some make sense
Others are pure nonsense
You will never be more
Than ink stains on a page
In a book
That will never be read again

I'm not sure you are worth
The fuss
Of the secrets
And hidden nights
Spent spilling desires
With agendas of reality
Not far behind those words
Spilled quickly across screens

I'm not sure I'm worth
The mess
Of the lies
You surely string about
When talking to her
About your day
And how much you missed her
While she looks lovingly into your eyes

I'm not sure we are worth
The pain
Or heartache
That comes from this twisted
Friendship we thought we had contained
Because we know better
Than everyone else
Who has ever done this before

I am often seduced by the darkness
That hides behind the eyes
Of people who seem so innocent

Some days it is hard to breathe... hard to smile... hard to just be here... knowing that you are all alone and there is no one in the world thinking of you in a way that you want to be thought about.

She decided to let the darkness take her. Leaving no trace of the person she once was. It was the only way to survive the pain of being alone.

I lost myself for a little while trying to forget all about you.

I have tried to forget your name, but there are so many things that remind me of you. Each one calling you out and into my memories.

I hate that you made me feel something
Despite my internal refusal to do so
And my wanting to stay hidden
My heart tugged in places
That my mind knew better
Than to wander off into

I burn in places where I once felt butterflies
I toil in places where I once felt pleasure
There is no end to this torture
There is no end to this loneliness
I once dreamed of your love
I once dreamed of your flesh
Now there is nothing
Now there is nothing

I have beat many addictions in my life... I can quit you too.

At the end of the day there is nothing but blood in my veins and a desire for it to be filled with something other than this loneliness.

I do not exist in a reality where love lands easily on my doorstep. I'm not even sure love can exist in my world.

You were my Nebraska. Boring, flat, and I had to go through you to get to where I really wanted to be.

You were never meant for me to love. Just another lesson I needed to learn.

I smell your death... as if it were my own. Your inability to love is killing me.

There is a suffering that speaks to anyone longing to be felt by another. Your mind wanders, and you catch yourself lost in thoughts. It seems to be the only thing left because there is no one in reality reaching to hold you.

I have tried many times to speak to you, but I cannot find the words. Every day I write thousands of words about things that do not matter. Yet simple words to form a sentence to you seem to escape me. Every damn time. Every fucking day. I have simply stopped trying.

I disappeared behind your shadow. Forgot how to be myself. An unrecognized reflection looking back at me. A tainted image. Damaged and broken pieces cutting away at me. Scars hidden away, ashamed. Covered up lies and secrets... for someone like you.

Don't forget to kiss the night as you walk through the darkness. Love your demons for making you who you are today... stronger, wiser, and braver.

I'm an echo falling to the floor
No matter how loud
Nor how long I scream
I am never truly heard

There isn't enough darkness to hide inside.

Cover my body deep in love
For the darkness has become too much
I can no longer handle any of it

It felt like a pin prick
Tiny
Not worth mentioning
It felt like a knife wound
Deeper
Hurting with every breath
It felt like dying
Buried
Gasping for air
Then it felt like nothing
Numb
Void of everything about you

It is in the silence that I have learned a thousand lessons.

Silent Kingdom

ABOUT THE AUTHOR

The author EB Allen has been writing poetry since the age of 15. She immediately fell in love with how it made her feel. She has not put her pen down since then. The name EB Allen is a pen name derived from parts of the authors real name and part of a family name. The author wishes to keep their anonymity a bit with their writings. Perhaps one day she will feel the need to come forward with her real name, but for now she is more comfortable being known by just this pen name when writing poetry.

Peace and Love,
EB Allen